I0142643

THE FIREMAN'S DAUGHTER

Jonathan Kinsman (he/him) is a bisexual, polyamorous, trans writer who was born in greater manchester in 1993. raised church of england and with a background in theological study he lives his life marrying his spirituality and his sexuality. he is a slam champion and received a distinction for his ma in creative writing at the university of sheffield. find him online @manykinsmen.

Also by Jonathan Kinsman

Genderfux [w/ Jem Henderson & JP Seabright]   (Nine Pens, 2022)

Witness   (Burning Eye Books, 2020)

&   (Indigo Dreams, 2018)

The Fireman's Daughter

Jonathan Kinsman

Broken Sleep Books

© 2023 Jonathan Kinsman. All rights reserved; no part of this book may be reproduced by any means without the publisher's permission.

ISBN: 978-1-915760-22-7

The author has asserted their right to be identified as the author of this Work in accordance with the Copyright, Designs and Patents Act 1988

Cover designed by Aaron Kent & Joe Kent

Edited by Kit Ingram

Typeset by Aaron Kent

Broken Sleep Books Ltd
Rhydwen
Talgarreg
Ceredigion
SA44 4HB

Broken Sleep Books Ltd
Fair View
St Georges Road
Cornwall
PL26 7YH

for dad,
who taught me how to be a man,

and in loving memory of my grandad, peter ashworth,
who taught me how to tie my shoelaces.

Contents

IGNITION

FLASHOVER

BACKDRAUGHT

DECAY

there is a last supper in every poem, which says: this is my body, here and now. and you know what comes next: passions, crucifixions, executions. others would also say resurrection…

—*jacques derrida*

IGNITION

a chemical reaction of heat, oxygen and a fuel source, resulting in a fire

a search party gathers after dark

it is the season of dead emperors
and they are pulling bodies out of you again
with the faithlessness of people
who have seen god come and leave.
now they only care for the cold,
mud soaking into their shoes.
they bring cigarettes and flasks full of whiskey
because they know the night will be long,
meandering towards the conclusion
of a beam of torch-light falling across
a set of stiff fingers or perhaps
the concaved back of a skull grown over
with hair like moss across a stone.

you no longer hold them in baptism;
you have become an unforgiving thing.

on nights like these i see the hills sideways,
the valley your gaping mouth,
your breath on my bare legs.
there's a pulse through the grass.
i have counted the steps between here
and the train tracks, the thrum of the river.
sometimes every light blows overhead
that marks the journey home
and the fields watch with their dark horses
and for a moment you sound
like someone calling in the distance,
the beat of their footsteps against the path;

or a hand reaching up from the water;
or a chasm opening inside the earth.

ars poetica

after jim steinman's love and death and an american guitar

i will tell you everything.
i will speak in precise details as if this is how it really happened:
i was virgin as a fresh page and i once killed a poem with a ballpoint pen.
i don't remember if it was a villanelle or an epic
but i do remember the sudden gush of inky menarche.
i don't remember if it was an ode or an apology
but i do remember the words tumbling over the cliff of my lips,
these hunks of sweating meat requiring
reassembly as i stitched the monster into being.
my hands hemorrhaged, a blasphemous stigmata,
and the blood was a spray of pomegranate seeds.
the blood of my hands was a feeding frenzy in the underworld.
my hands took the lord's name in vein
and i could form words never even spoken before.
so i took my hands and i wrote about the prime minister;
i wrote about fields of dead rabbits;
i wrote about alcoholic mountaineers;
wrote about unsatisfying orgasms;
wrote about fucking a medical student.
the medical student curled his hand around his cock.
the poem curled its arms around its wounded belly
and i ran back to my house on the top of the hill.
mummy and daddy were eating at the kitchen table.
starved, i salivated over the hardwood floors,
carved up splinters all the way to my seat.
i flung open my notebook
and just as i was about to sign another black mark on the page,
teeth squealing through a thick slice of back bacon,
my father looked up and grunted *tell me —*
i need to understand. tell me something — you're the writer.
how do you know when a poem is finished?

and i said: *goddammit daddy.*
you know i love you, but you have a hell of a lot to learn about editing.

45rpm

heart block is a slowness or abnormality in the heart's rhythm due
to a fault in its electrical conduction system
tread wrong here and the needle jumps —
skrt-skrt-skrt. iggy pop plays the songs
on christmas day, picks from discs
wrinkled as his skin and john lydon

flogs butter all gussied up and english
gentleman; tells you what proper means
like getting on is getting out and that's the rub.

beat

overnight, your heart rate
registers seventeen beats per minute —
takes a rest of five whole seconds.

do you feel it, the slowing?
or does it lurch like a record played at the wrong speed?
jo-leeeeene, a drunk clutches a table,
fingers the vinyl, begs the spin stop.
beat
all these revolutions coming back around,
change and change again, until your knees ache,
your back bent with all this wisdom,

and i am seven inch and stupid,
hopped up on song,
like you were back when punk was young.
i am my father's son

beat

till sick with hope,
proud as oak that breaks before it gives.

they set the pacemaker to forty-five —
do you remember how, when the time came,
you sold your singles, settled down?

come on dad, once more with feeling.
call me fool again and mean it.

my mother is buying me a bra

that fits.

something that won't
        leave welts under my arms.

it'll feel so soft, so easy,
i'll wear it on weekends too,
                    forget it's there,
                    she promises.

in the changing room, the tape
measure nicks against my nipples
with its sharp fine edge
in glancing blows, counts
with clinical distance the difference
between bust and ribs. her

hands are cold as a corpse's.
they cup my bosom so tenderly.
she says *buxom* is a gift,
traces in etymology *obedience,*
does not press.

a good bra
        will let me breathe.

three dreamscapes

i.

we go down to the beachfront,
somewhere from my childhood – rhyl, perhaps
        cleaned up for a film set
        a deeper blue than i remember, lit by night,
and you touch me in the fag-ash sand.

    the water crinkles under foot
        when we walk out to touch the painted-on horizon
   that powders against thumb.
            i say *i think i always knew*
      and sit facing you when i straddle your thighs,
           my eyes on the seawall and its white railings
    expecting an audience that never turns up,

my hips in dutiful motion
    until you cry out *no*
            and a pair of thick arms
               drag me away.

ii.

i haven't acted since i was thirteen
        but still you say *i loved you as wendy,*
  not knowing i only ever played a lost boy,
               and the kids in their little black leotards file out
     as you waltz me across the floor.

              maybe we're upstairs in some pub in the peaks
                 or maybe it's the church hall,
            the wood slick with polish
              and the buzzing bar-lights reflected in it
                     like suns.

i've been told dancing is a metaphor
        and this time i'm good at it –
   my body happening to someone else
            in spins and lifts and clutches close to the chest
      your breath leaning into mine

             while the director claps from his chair.

iii.

you look at me across the garden party and say
　　we're the perfect couple
　while i pull up fistfuls of grass, plait the blades together.
i can see my house from here,
　　over the heads of all your blonde cousins.
　　　　　i need air.

　　i don't know if anyone has a greenhouse anymore
　　　　but still i go there, walk among the basil and the
tarragon,
　　feel the leaves against my cheeks, my ankles,
　　　　how they stroke as you lift my sundress
　and take me there, face pressed to the hot floor tiles,
　　the pattern printing my skin as i grasp at the glass panes,

tell you i hate you,
　　i want to go home.

birthday candles

look closely now,
    can you see her, there in the flame?
            a swaying charcoal dancer,
                    her arms raised high
                in the ecstatic conflagration,
    this pink and white spiral staircase
  collapsing beneath her,
      and across the glazed skyline
        every tower goes up in reverence,
                    the darkness alight with song
                        babylon burning
                    for your sake.
            don't think of your father
            ascending floor after floor
      wax ceilings collapsing
  over his shoulders
    sweet powder in his eyes as he
            searches, sugar in his lungs.
                he's here, match pinched
            between finger and thumb,
        laughing through
            a flat happy birthday.
                dear amy,
                make a wish.

this is gonzo dream pornography,
not forty winks erotica

with thanks to sam j. grudgings for the title

my nightmind, bored of its metaphors,
    summons your face
or else a mask near enough
i could mistake it
       in this cheap hotel room,

(its pink brick
       says *homosexuals welcome*, its blue door
          especially policemen)
   as you take down your work trousers,
    command me *eat.*

and I do, thick with drool,
grunt in it,
   lick the feral taste of your sweat
    from your flesh,
  waif at the banquet table.
    (arthouse would make this too beautiful; pornography miss
your grip on my wrists like jacob wrestling, the dante and virgil
back bend you make with your fist in my hair).

    let me devour every false detail
       the thick fur of your calves,
          the shapes in the pull of your abdomen,
 the storm of your muscles twitching
    beneath the skin's tension,

      (my wrong-sized nipples,
       like the nights i wear a borrowed skin to dream in while
some half-remembered fuck
  pulls on mine like a night gown.)

let this slip beneath the duvet's censor,
     you can't pause the tape
   to capture this moment.
        i conjure drag queens,
    contortionists.

   wear me out
  the way only someone
         who's already forgotten
 my name can.

i'll rise slow tomorrow,
     slink to my work-desk still damp.

     like a premonition,
    stranger-love, do you come?

death of a boyband

that's it then. the band broke up
    and offer now
        a pill for the small griefs:

   some twee malady;
      some distant smile played on repeat;
    those soft doe-eyes dust-sheeted
as your love turns away.

       this is rehearsal,
     you learn,
        for the next performance.

candle snuffed
   so a bonfire knows how to burn itself out –
and you will mix the tincture
   just right when the moment arrives,
but for now you satisfy your need for hurt,
  some bubbling undercurrent not yet heard,
sobbing into lemonade.

 they're made to measure boys
    custom built to fill the hollow void as your hand
 first grasps the air.
     your choice of five, or six,
   to fit your preference.
     so you select a favourite,

       that first ache
     sugar spun
       from his lips,
         tooth-rot stuff.

it never lasts.
boyhood
   gives way to man,
  puppy fat undressed,
     how tease
      moves on to boldness
    and you dance along,
     a beat or two behind.

              they'll always leave you,
               outgrow the baby steps –
                    change their hair, their genre –
            pick up a guitar, an addiction, disappear.

   and it hurts
      at least as far as you can understand,
     tears on your pillow and all those grand clichés
          played out unironically
               as you rip the posters from the wall,
             snap cds over your skinny little knees,
        shriek and wail
          for their betrayal.

                  practice pain
               for the real thing.

iterations of self

for amy, who was

i.
self as inheritance:

your mother howls like it's the moon she's pushing out of her belly. sweating empress of the sky, she plants her feet in the bed, hair zephyred in the sheets. as with your father's birth, it's twins: a girl and a boy, amy & jonathan. unlike your father's birth, the two are identical. from your mother, eyes like a downpour. from your father, the occupation of the same space. on the drive home from the hospital, your father beats his hands against the steering wheel in time to a song by simon & garfunkel, his grin wide enough to swallow all six lanes.

ii.
self as augury:

king of cups, reversed. you are terrified of becoming your father, always fleeing, every articulation gone to the fire. the hierophant, reversed. we are taught a bloodline will bind us. the hanged man reversed. it won't. carry on turning your cards, see it: judgement. reversed. judgement. reversed. judgement. reversed.

iii.
self as electron:

contemplate the light, its red and its violet. consider the theories postulated by quantum mechanics: perhaps there is only one particle in all places at once. conclude that you were made in the dark.

iv.

self as repetition:

your grandfather cuts a barbed spiral of identical paper girls at the kitchen table. they push themselves up from the surface and arm in arm they go, singing *amy, amy* as they march eyelessly towards its edge. *what to do with all these little girls? there are so many of you, heaps upon heaps of you.* your grandfather is calling you by your mother's name and you don't have the strength to correct him as you sweep the scraps into your hand and begin to devour them.

v.

self as wendigo:

amy sharpens herself against the leather, the splintered bones of her desire made blade, her mouth a string of white pearls. *how long have i been eating myself?* her collections of teeth are grinding together in the jar as she assembles herself on the bed, twisting her limbs like an infant class construction of yoghurt pots and pipe-cleaners. the air groans through her tissue-paper skin, her face a self-portrait done in lipstick. *i've always been so determined to be monstrous.*

vi.

self as vanity:

they name you for love and the only thing you love is the sound of your own damn voice.

vii.
self as silhouette:

at the bathroom sink, jonathan watches tap-water as it falls through translucent fingers, tumbles into steam through the cups of his palms. *please somebody remind me of my hands.* he catches shape in the light, folding into rabbit, then dove, then barking dog with one paw extended, refracting himself inwards and inwards and inwards. *is this where i left them? grasping at water, playing over its surface, as if i know anything of thirst, of drowning.*

viii.
self as masturbation:

this is your third jonathan. have you fucked yourself enough yet to want something different?

ix.
self as femininity

fists full of keys, amy teaches herself righteous anger, how to shift tongue into dagger, straps a megaphone across her back like a quiver. *throw open your doors, else i'll lay siege, topple every tower, for when i speak even the stone stops to listen, even the stars still in the sky.* lady armoured red, queen of rioters and highwaymen, striding fearless down the centre of the street unconcerned by motor engines. *pink is what happens when you water down women.*

x.
self as masculinity

fingers raised to feel the breeze, jonathan tracks barefoot through the fells, content to let the clouds pass overhead uninterrupted. he spins with the slow rotation of the planet, carves lichtenberg figures into the hillside, chalk scars on the landscape, scent of thunder, voice of autumn leaves. *all these things invisible: the hand that lifts the bumblebee, the eyelids that slide closed into night, the thoughts that write the world.*

xi.
self as hallucination:

mirror images tap the glass of their reflections, meet at the conjecture of amy's daggered nails and jonathan's calloused fingertips, each poised to beg for their existence. *pray tell, which of us is you?*

xii.
self as deity:

a condemned cathedral grown over with vines, its innards open to the sky but the stained glass still spilling all the colours of light onto the floor. deer hooves against that old stone as they cross the altar. silent communion. birds overhead, weaving branches from the air. jonathan sitting, hands folded, in the last pew. *everything, everything.* and amy beside him, her fingers in his hair, priestess of earth. *who are we that demand understanding? none of us will be spared.*

xiii.

self as ampersand:

only say the word. body and name, each of these are yours to unmake and make again from their constituent dust. even gods have built imperfectly, creeping towards completion. look at us.

FLASHOVER

a near-simultaneous ignition of directly-exposed combustible material in an enclosed area. temperatures reach one thousand degrees fahrenheit

anton yelchin

i am thinking of a dent in a set of iron railings;
how the bend backwards still aches in the struts
as if, even now, these bars are straining
to pull away from their wrought framework,

the spine's final, awful contortion.
they're reporting that he was an actor, a young man
with kiss-curl hair and dimpled cheeks, still keen
to talk about stanislavski. they're printing his face
in an oval beside a photograph of the damaged fence,
and i am thinking of him pinned there like a butterfly,
his lungs fluttering in the darkness. they're saying it
probably took a full minute and asking what he was
thinking stood there with the engine running.
perfect posture. isadora duncan. nobody's watching.

freak accident, they're calling it,
and i am thinking of how some things
can creep up on you, like a jeep rolling
backwards down the drive,
whilst you're facing the other way.

bloodhound

i.

at fifteen, my body comes in all at once —
          all that raw flesh where only bones were.
          the changing room echoes wet
                          with tongues licking chops.
          make no mistake,
        girls are carnivores
                        and this is starving season.

          i fix my gaze on the floor
    as the girls growl
            under their moistened breaths
                    don't you dare. don't you fucking dare bitch,
        my heartbeat rabbit fast,
                    skin flushed rarest pink
                            against white cotton underwear,
                bottom of the class,
                last across the line.

                        they wait for my mistake,
                            a slip of a foot on the wet floor,
              and they'll grasp me by the hair
                        make me bare
                          my throat in supplication,

        salivate
          we can smell it on you.

ii.

at eighteen, we both know
    the swiftest way to seal a wound
               is with the mouth.
               your teeth break my skin;
a ring of blood at the nape of my neck
    (men span with fingers,
      but only your mark sinks so deep);
            my howl dies to a whimper
         smothered in your mother's sheets.

when i am vodka-blind,
    the dark moves as a pack of strange beasts,
            beckoning me home.
    your sober lips hush against my back
            and the bark behind the door
           i think that you can hear.

babe, don't leave me with my hands tonight
babe, tonight i've got this fear.

donkeyskin

i knew a boy, once,
      who wore a coat of donkeyskin
      clutched tight about him,

         let it slip from his shoulders only in bedrooms,
                 darkened auditoriums —

stretched it taut and thin
      over everything,

        turned the stars in the heavens
     to broken glass on blacktop,
          begged nightly for the lord
          to bless him with ugly children,

              kissed me softy,

          cried *beautiful.*
            oh god, you're so beautiful.

ghost sonnet for my vanishing twin

i have been asked *do you hate what you must be?* as if we are anything but ghostly –
these dark rooms confession booths, interrogation cells, our bodies in stasis.
i knew a woman once who clung on just long enough to hear the entire discography of david bowie.
these are strange things that matter. i am collapsing in on myself between spaces.
my father gasps when the voice on the radio says she didn't know she was a twin,
clutches my aunt's hand to his chest, compresses those miles of distance to a heartbeat.
in bed together, warm and sightless, i can turn this blanket to a membrane stretched thin.
when we curl face to face, i picture him, that absent other part, your touch celestial heat.
i need to know you love me like this, when unlived he twitches in my skin as lost hours,
that skeleton boy, his face double-exposed upon mine in the flash of your eyes
and broken down to nothing in a sudden rush of blood. i could watch endless meteor showers,
burn each and every wish on nonexistence and still return to these comfortable lies.
can you hear it in the silence? how even my name dies in the void of my mouth.
how he reaches through my throat. how his wails echo in our hollow. *let me out. let me out.*

it's like this

i.
it's like this:

two of your lovers stand before you. the one on the left you can look in the eye with relative ease. the one on the right has you bending backwards until your spine is almost folded in half just to meet his gaze. your mother would prefer the one on the right, regardless of his indiscretions, which are far worse than those of the one on the left. the one on the right has sharp, green eyes that prefer fiction to reality. the one on the left has recently complimented your eyes, the first in a long time to see the ring of hazel around the pupil that is swallowed by dilation, so he is winning. your pupils are not currently dilated.

ii.
it's like this:

two of your lovers stand before you. the one on the left has broad shoulders and a narrow waist that form the inverted triangle used to illustrate the ideal male form. you know every inch of him, every purple stretch mark flying as a tattered flag from the mast of his spine, his arthritic knees, the twist of his nose where it broke and set wrong. the one on the right is a woman. you have never once touched her, but still you know every millimetre of flesh, every maroon stria skirting like bloodied fingers over the swell of her hips, her twitching muscles, the palpations of her arrhythmic heart. the one on the left you've known since childhood, pictured his soft blonde hair and wide cheekbones as the details in the miniscule illustrations of your bedtime reading. the one on the right you've known all your adult life. she is dark and seen only as a creature emerging from shadows. in order to determine the winner, both of them tell you a secret. one of them tells only you.

iii.
it's like this:

two of your lovers stand before you. neither of them you see anymore. both of them have mostly forgotten you ever existed, except for the odd occasion when you post a really good selfie. while examining it on their phone, they will both lean back and congratulate themselves on having had sex with you. the winner is the first to like said selfie. the one on the left hurt you only once, but deeply, like a headsman with an almost sharp axe. the one on the right hurt you in a sustained volley of gunfire over the course of several years. you snort as their names rise in your notifications. you wonder if they realise you have let them both go.

iv.
it's like this:

two of your lovers stand before you. one of their respective cocks you prefer. when they ask about it, you will tell both of them that you meant theirs. you'll be lying. the winner is you.

v.
it's like this:

two of your lovers stand before you. both of them spent a substantial part of their formative years on the island of nassau but they have never met before now. the one on the left moved away a long time ago. for the one on the right, that wound is still fresh. the mother of the one on the left will say *are you a lesbian* with an honest indifference. the mother of the one on the right will say *an english girl* with an indifference that must be practiced. your mother will say *are you sure you want to be with someone like that* in a tone that reveals she likes neither of them. the winner is everyone's mother.

vi.
it's like this:

two of your lovers stand before you. the one on the left is the first person you ever loved though you only know this in retrospect. the one on the right you recently realised you are in love with. the winner is whoever's name is the first out of your mouth. both of them are women with scrutinising gazes whose eyes glisten with mania through their curtains of dark hair. both of them lower their deep, brassy voices. somebody turns off the light. all of you are counting the seconds.

vii.
it's like this:

you are having a threesome with two of your lovers, both of them men, both of them avoiding looking the other in the eye. one above, one below, the two of them are locked in a tug of war over the spine of your being. the pressure builds. you cry out *i don't bend like that*, but they continue as if they have not heard. your bones splinter at sacrum and coccyx. you snap in two. the winner is the one holding the larger part.

viii.
it's like this:

two of your lovers stand before you. neither of them know that the other is your lover. all three of you sit down to play a drinking game. you are sweating. one sits on your left and the other on your right. the one on the left is drinking awful, mass-produced lager made by a non-european company. the one on the right is drinking craft ale from a local brewery and is feeling pretty smug about it. across from you is sitting your third lover, whom everyone knows about, drinking tequila neat. it is her turn. she says *never have i ever slept with her*. all of them drink. technically, you win.

ix.

it's like this:

two of your lovers are putting their tongues down each other's throats in front of you. part of you thinks *fuck, that's hot*. part of you carries on drinking regardless. part of you twists your torso over the side of the sofa and vomits. part of you thinks *they make a cute couple*. part of you turns to your third lover with a raised eyebrow. part of you is roaring *it should be me, only me*. part of you gazes out of the open front door. the winner is the part you feed.

x.

it's like this:

two of your lovers stand before you. both of them are terrible in bed and therefore losing. two more of your lovers are standing over to one side conversing in murmurs you can't quite translate. the one on the left is wearing clown make-up. the one on the right is a clown. both raise their eyebrows at you, open their arms and beckon. you expel the other two. both cry a little and you attempt to comfort them but ultimately make everything worse. *clownfucker*, the one on the left spits at you as he leaves. the one on the right says nothing but you can see betrayal in his eyes. you say *the best trait a person can have is taking instruction well*. you're lying, it's humour. you go to bed with your remaining lovers.

xi.

it's like this:

two of your lovers stand before you. they are similarly featured, as if playing to some eugenics propaganda you cannot subscribe to. both of them are strong enough to hold you aloft and trembling above their heads. both leave finger-shaped bruises along the tops of your thighs that you are quietly pleased to find afterwards. both of them are their fathers' sons, so alike in quirking eyebrows, their gazes filtered down their noses. the one on the left promises he will never hurt you and does not yet know that he is lying. the one on the right says that he might, but then again, he only might. both of them your mother would like for she does not know their indiscretions. the loser is the first to catch himself in the urge to strike you.

xii.

it's like this:

you are at an orgy of all your potential lovers. across the apocalypse of bodies, you recognise his face, but don't know where you know it from. he radiates a soft light that has your feet flying across the flesh floor before you. it does not matter who you stand on, they are too absorbed in one another. you touch his face. he looks like what might happen if angels bleached their hair. a band of pearls forms a circlet around his head. *i am dreaming*, you say, eyes travelling over impossibly smooth skin in the knowledge that this face of his is only borrowed. *of course, but we have time,* he replies. you rest your head against his naked chest. his fingers smooth over your hair. you begin to cry and both of you know all the reasons for it. around you, each of them reaches orgasmic bliss. in this regard, everyone's a winner, but inside one another, none of them are closer than the two of you pressed together like this. they descend. *out of time, i'm sorry.* he wraps his arms over you like a bed of feathers as they begin to eat him, every muscle and sinew, painting each other in the splatter of his organs. a woman turns to you. she has a string of pearls dangling limply between her teeth. as you ascend violently to consciousness, you recognise the face as that of a popular singer. you put on one of his songs. you bring yourself off.

xiii.
it's like this:

two of your parents stand before you. freud is having a field day. the one on the left is your father, who is wearing his wedding ring because it is a sunday and part of the proper dress for church. the one on the right is your mother, whose wedding ring is stuck on her finger and has been for years. at this stage in his life, most of the people your father works with are women. your mother jokingly refers to them as your father's harem. at this stage in her life, your mother doesn't work away from home as much as she once used to. after church, your mother packs for london. your father does the washing up. your mother kisses your father on the lips and says *goodbye, darling.* the winner is everyone's place of employment.

xiv.
it's like this:

you are standing in a colosseum watching all of your previous lovers fight to the death. each member of the ten thousand people that make up the audience is a potential lover in a potential universe. not everyone has a sword. not everyone has a net. some of your lovers are pacifists. some of your lovers are pushing their faces down into the dirt. *say the word. say the word and i let them live. turn your thumb.* you are holding your hand at the level of your eye. the sky is blue, as always. the ground is red, as always. the crowd is growing restless, as always, and are beginning to undress, beginning to touch mouth to mouth, hand to naked breast, hand to genitalia. no one looks you in

the eye, consumed in the moment, in desire. *decide the winner. choose.*
you raise your hand to your crown of laurels, take it from your head
and set it down.

how to walk on water

*since 2007, at least twenty detached human feet have been found on the
coasts of the salish sea, though instances go back more than a century*

you'll need the
appropriate footwear,

        usually a sneaker —

            a vaporfly for the long-distance runner,

        or perhaps a pair of air jordans,

    — but in a pinch,

        any old hiking boots will do.

                trust them to hold you

              tighter than yourself

        and begin to empty the body

        from your body.

the water chooses the destination —

    a head rolls onto the isle of whithorn;

        a weathered femur with its vinegar tan

buried in the sand of new south wales;

long island is a favourite for torsos

tattooed with peaches and cherries,

flesh taking notes

from the coconut,

conducting trials for

propagation by sea

— but it's the feet that make shore most

often and increasingly frequent,

cradled in a memory foam insole,

as if the act requires

diminishing faith.

levothyroxine
for sol

on a wistful morning like this, i empty your bottled time
into the cup of my palm, press the pearl of salvation
against your tongue as if communion wafer. i can't quite
imagine the details: the surgeon elbow-deep in your belly
becomes your own hands in the soil, repotting a banana tree.

i tell you *if it all ends tomorrow, we'll raid the pharmacy;*
we'll plant a garden; we'll keep ticking over.

i tell you *if it all ends tomorrow, we'll divide you evenly*
among us; all of us will eat; not a bite will go to waste.

cosmonaut

from the front step,
  my grandfather watches the sky
     for something going up,

   while the old dog next-door remembers
     his howl,

thinks of gagarin
     lighting the vast darkness,
  a struck match,

   the cruelness of making him go alone,

squints at the stars, waits

     until the dog quiets.

whatever he's looking for
just keeps getting further away.

   he sighs,
    turns once more
   to the empty rooms
     of his house.

my great-grandfather drops dead while conducting a séance at auntie christine's wedding

think of it as a trick and you'll get no response.
manning the switchboard, dials drifting beneath
trickling out of the headset and into the room, a soup of it
through the glazed-in drapes. you are patching through
in another calling code. *hello? hello? i have*
someone whose name begins with a
you wouldn't do this, not again, not today.
and you've the cheek to play at conjuring the dead.
still remember your last disappearing act and
as a television playing in another room,
the six o'clock news bubbled up
scrambled cypher of rotted minds.

instead, you imagine yourself
your hands, a fog of static
                                            strained
       to a citizen
a message waiting for
j... you promised
a good catholic wedding
                              the kids
these voices come through
      terse and clipped,
             across time,

and the words are always the same: *forgive me,*

please forgive me.

51

gravedigger

believing a man may only suffer death once,
he churns the soil for fresh bones
like a mother feeds her stock over the fire after supper,
bare hands to the bloody blankets.

someone must make this journey for them,
even with half-remembered rites,
stagger back from the graveside in the bile and dirt.
make no mistake, the digger is no ferryman.

he takes a watch, a gold tooth, a wedding band,
or else the earth returns it for his pay,
while the town sweats death from every house,
his own family a monstrous knot of flesh

carried on his back as he staggers from his doorstep,
spine lilting beneath their weight,
and still he lifts his spade to bury, every name
he's ever learnt interred in earth.

ask any orpheus, he'll tell
the worst of hell is returning from it.

BACKDRAUGHT

occurring in fires that are not ventilated, a sudden explosion caused by introducing more oxygen into a fire that has consumed its initial supply

overture con sordina

for s., no apology is enough

i.

in the beginning was the word
and the word was

NO

ii.

and from it life sang like iron
through the guts

the cut and thrust

retched
forth in the wet slap
of bile against water

iii.

all the earth perched upon your cervix
how you trembled under its weight

we of infinite recursion
nesting dolls
ground at your insides

iv.

waiting for the break

star gasp
the blade that split
the shell

dripping yolk

you cannot make
anything without

v.

grit
you polished your ache
and it shines
blinding

vi.

a body a promise
and the nations cried
if you cannot keep it to yourself
we will keep it for you

crowned the babe with paper
blank verse

severed

vii.

and the child wailed winter

alone
on the mountaintop

my stone mother
a scream a scarecrow

howled the hangman
and his wife

bent double beneath the empty

viii.

madonna
we call her now
a precious thing

and you
my grandmother of the road ahead
our lady of ringing bells
queen under the earth

ix.

i lower my voice to you
whisper in the bloody dirt

hymn umbilical

x.

name me clock
and i will wind back his hands

stop time
unspeak

great are the mysteries of faith

god looks ruinous tonight,
     eyes alive
          and amber in
               grasping flamelight,

   lifts them from the earth
      to meet you,
              this youth
           with wine-dark lips
   and voice that aches with song,
        prostrate
          in some muddy sheep field,

i'm sorry i've been such a tyrant,
    a regular caligula,

  gives permission,
   spreads those limbs,
        a plucked dove,

   your mouths of want
              descending
    to snap the wishbone,
 suck ribs clean of meat,
the flesh giving off its own light,

        Κύριε, ἐλέησον
       gurgled in blood.

werewulf

how many nights
            beneath god's milk-white left eye

        to become
                    to howl?

we stuck things are
            creatures
                    not seen as we should be,

    fixed under your gaze.

mother, bring me my funeral suit
                    my black winter coat.

        let's bury my womb
                grant it rest
                    in this piece of earth.

call me by my blue name.
    slip *jonathan* from your lips
            as if it means *love*

                — because mama it does.

immolations

you fell in love with the fireman's daughter,
                          and i'm sorry for your misplaced faith.
        this will protect you no more
than sigils traced on playing fields
by children running through the mist.

        (this is a harsh place.
              in summer the moors burn.
              everything on foot turns to the water,
        collects in the reservoir, live debris,
                    and the earth churns up blackened bones
              that crumble to ash in your hands:
                  the smallest of femurs; neat little skulls
                            set with milk teeth,
    but it's winter's bite that's deepest.)

do you remember our bare legs pink in the frost?
how every snowflake scalded our skin?
        or the day we were turned back by panicked teachers,
      melting plastic reaching our nostrils
                  slower than burning flesh?

                  (a man rises at dawn
                              with divine calm
                          and walks onto oldham edge,
                        with a carton full of petrol
                              and a pack of cigarettes.
                  his eyes burst like yolks,
                        run down his face as tears.
                              he takes his medication —
                          does not even scream.)

it was so cold then,
                    huddled together like sheep,
            your hands clutching for warmth,
            ice on every breath, bodies grown numb
                and year on year it returns:

                    i am frightened of who we are in winter.
                        i am frightened of what we will burn.

otesanek (greedy guts)

anything can be a child, if you squint,

so they swaddle the swollen stump,
bind its leaves up in bunches,
set it out in the garden
in a little pink sunhat

even as it weeps

its gnarled fat fists beating against
mother's breast, its fissure mouth
clamped tight, refuses to suckle
until the surgeon cuts a wider
wooden grimace to force the teat inside.

milk, its only word,

screams *milk milk milk*
and snatches up the neighbour's cat,
sicks bloody froth against the muslin
that first tooth a nasty splinter
sunk tight in *pussy pussy pussy.*
its chest warps, distends and yowls,
so father sits it upside-down

says *you have had*

your pretty pussy, settle, fucking settle
but now the stump has the colic
sets upon the paperboy,
a perfect little beast that fills the throat
as he goes down and a cry goes up of

paper boy milk boy pussy boy
while all its writhing branches crack
to burst its frilly dresses,
ribbons, lace and thread
meant to bind this whitsun demon
tattered on the lawn
and it sprints naked for the gate, needs

a taste of flesh

to satiate the hunger before it thinks
of sleep but daddy's got the axe out,
shrieks *we'll have ourselves a bonfire*
and gives chase about the garden
while mummy sits and sobs
for the child she wanted
and not the child she got.

now

he's barbequing dinner
and she's digging out a stone
a lump of orange brick buried
in the flowerbed and she
swaddles this instead
says *this one's a son, love.*

at least we're not alone.

a prayer of st gertrude

for toby

you can carry
holy water in a
jam jar sealed
with   wax
paper, like the
priest   does,
tight   to   her
chest,   all
through   the
hills

without you,

& if this is god's
house maybe it
is vacant &

the   darkness
has no edges.

the food on the
table   rotted
down to dust.

after sundown,
when   she
comes to mark
our house.

i hold you like a
candle.

& if this is the
room
set   aside   for
me

it   is   not   its
hands that

let the door be
unbolted &

if the spirit
rots, you'll
smell it,   grasp me but   let me leave it.
                          its infinite face,
                          eyes   carved
                          clean   from
                          sockets,

she   says,   *it*
turns like milk.

                                                & if no one else
                                                is coming

i give you the
last of it.   mouth
                           stretched
                           wide

you'll   take   all
the god
you can get.   with silence.

                           distance is only
                           wax.   – please stay.

                           time   is   only
                           light.   please   god,
                                                please stay.

all things, always

for grandad john

when you were now
            and here
            all possible futures   stretched before you

                                    as a box of matches

            and inside each
            of them
                        side by side
                                    ashen   and   spent.

my father

sixteen
    and sixty his hair

                                    grey and knees
                                    scraped   and you

in the bed

                        a little boy

                        abandoned again to the
                    whims of these

                                            arguing voices

to forget your   shame you must abandon all of it
each   visitor
                                    resurrecting   the dead
                grandchildren
                        growing backwards to

unbirth

so a son

might   once again   take breath
your   voice   shrinks away   language dying

in the blankets

with every   disappointment
all of this
quantum

memory stacked   upon   itself

until
time
collapses

and takes
meaning
with it

what we   observe
is a
fraction
of a
fraction
your mind

the soup

of great
cosmic

insignificance how

like a god

this man in the bed

this ancient

frail monolith

scrubbed clean

of its sins

looks upon his creation
and

does

not

recognise

it

antares is thinking of ending things

each dusk i wake heavier   and drag my cast-
iron belly over the horizon's bloated lip.

in   babylon,   i   was   a   goddess.
masochists,   adoration-drunk,   slit
their own throats.

now, i lose weeks to my
bed,   my   bonfires
outshone by the meagre
sun of an obscure galaxy.

i   dream
apocalypse: my
skin   split,   ribs
unfurled,
scorpion   pulse
measuring   the
last

(orgasm)

BOMBS.

in nuclear

CLIT

my bright

will **throb**

in the sky for weeks,

a brand

the dark scar

in every retina,

of my departure.

hush darling,

it'll be over soon.

recovery

how do you imagine yourself now?

      odysseus among the flotsam,
  an ikea's worth of parts
         and no instructions?

         ithaca is not where you left it,
    though it tugs at the edge of your mouth,
  penelope's unbearable fidelity
    a fish-hook for you to asphyxiate upon.

is it still a victory if you don't make it home?

on the electrodynamics of moving bodies

to return from the dead requires
absolute darkness, so we, slavish
creatures of conventional physics,
seal the door, go home. and you
go nowhere, a fixed point to our
travelling, your electrons fallen
marbles decelerated to zero. it is
impossible to hold this nothingness
in our minds so we call it unknown,
assign it a continuous loop, figure it
as a cross mark in our summations.
the light knows nothing of what
it leaves behind, cannot change
direction, travels a fixed course
pushing infinitely onwards until
that sudden stop in which it scatters,
illuminates and we are seen, particles
of dust caught in this momentary
radiance, beings of pure time. let it
unwind, the universe unravelling,
entire planets loosed from gravity
tumbling in free fall through endless
space as a finger trails through chalk,
unbalances the equation, erases
to undo this mistake. to return
from the dead requires absolute
darkness, each of us trudging toward
tomorrow, all hope lost.

DECAY

when all fuel and oxygen has been consumed, the fire slowly goes out

flamborough head

we're an hour out of dodge
when i realise

we have no reason
to trust each other,

just the promise of the coastline
on a clear august day.

i watch your profile,
your gaze obscured,

the shape of your words.
i want you in this way

that feels like dread.
lead me down the stairs,

take me to the shorefront,
the lighthouse at our backs,

to the sharp, cold water,
neither of us certain,

when i ask
is the tide going out

or coming in?

elegy for a broken condom

sunday morning,
       three of us make this pilgrimage,
     watch you configure the if-then
        of our genitals, like a puzzle box full of spunk.

o till operator,
who forgives all with 15.99,
i commend to you this fallen latex —

i know my lines.
  in your privacy room,
    my catholic ancestors betray me
  when i pray *thank you lord for making my pussy*
            vice-like and bizarrely angled,
with pill on my tongue,
  take the proffered cup
      to cleanse my gums.

  temple of medicine,
i beg miracles:

    i bring you
boys with heart conditions,
   philosophers and statisticians,
       men who pay,
    who buy extra-safe,
      fuck like the charge of the light brigade.

pharmacist forgive us our pleasure,
politician lead us not into legislation,
gp deliver us from foetus.

cross my fingers,
       hold my breath.

            i've read the booklet,
    when science doesn't know
        it makes a guess.

subjective vision hypothesis

wake with the widows,
tread the path up to the cemetery
in the rough morning light,
crush wildflowers underfoot.

if there is anything beautiful left,
it ought to be ashamed of itself,
daffodils springing from buried husbands
foxgloves towering over the stillborn,
curse their colours,
insipid yellow, pompous purple,

this concrete mausoleum
a canopic jar broken open
for even a pinch of divinity.

but enter in,
hear the impossible rush
of water beneath,
the grave opening to a vast chasm
no candle illuminates,
casket grown to fruiting tree
that bows its branches,
doffs its crown of blossom,

not here, but risen,

creaked as a fig falls
that sweetest flesh offered up to you,
the squelch and the crunch,
wasp-corpse stings the lips

that move for alleluia
as the wood burns.

nothing returns as it once was,
but still, it returns.

transitional art forms

i.
michelangelo, 1475–564

the great artist can't get the breasts right.
anyone would think he never nursed upon a teat.
the boy clutches sweet oranges to his bare chest,
a pair, fat with juice, exotic, strange, costly,
and mocking as he poses beside the marble.
he's right, these are too round, too sparse,
an afterthought on a chiselled torso that
never wept for milk in a woman's flesh,
and this boy is not oranges but miles of vineyards
stretched out before the eye, sheets of
dripping honeycomb, fresh bread and olive oil.
say *leonardo painted himself. a clean shave and*
a woman's shawl but the smile is unmistakable
and clutch him close. slip hands beneath
the fruit, prise them from his body, let him gasp,
watch them tumble, roll beneath the cupboards,
gather dust. still he laughs, a coy look, retorts
and michelangelo lay upon his back to paint his lord.

ii.
pope pius ix, 1846 –1878

piss flows from the wound. when god stretched out
a hand and carved creation, he made this too.
it was the lord's idea to have the cock and still man
made cloth, stitched sin in the fig's leaves,
took a knife to his design. roll those papal plums
between finger and thumb, watch this dutiful mutilation,

cardinal desires, iconoclasm. you like them sexless, crying
dust, broken boys, those small, soft things locked away
for only men with self-control to view, to touch.
and still the throne demands it, give us christian
foreskin to rub as relic, give us manna to suck
from the wellspring, let god come upon us through you,
statues bleeding gold in the path of the chisel.
turn your thumb, watch apollo's ritual castration,
grasp the trophy: smooth, beautiful youth.
filth, you say, *insidious idolatry, poison of the eye.*
he does not flinch, refuses to play pygmalion.
his holiness' jurisdiction does not extend to hell.

iii.
jonathan, 2019–present

the boy studies the masters, learns their tricks.
he presses shadows along the cut of his jaw,
carves something angular, proud to match the arc
of his brow, his broad shoulders; maps out a cleft;
factures his hairline; scatters light across his cheekbone;
traces the downward trajectory of his nose into
a cherubic pout. he paints in titian blue, rembrandt red
against his paleness. his eye falls on hips, on chest,
imagines the block before him, waiting to understand
his vision in its cold stone. what next? a masterpiece
takes years of work and he is impatient in his wait,
his body twisting in its bonds. he weeps free me
from this flesh that my image might take flight.
each day it falls away, the sculptor at the cell bars
grinds and loosens. a chisel, a file, a scalpel,
a prescription, until one fine morning he will see
himself at last amidst the dust of what was not.
the art is in the scar, knowing what to take away.

some possible genders

ballboy / girl guide / motherfucker / ratking / her majesty / emcee / ladykiller / ex-lover / godfather / grave cleric / cock-jokey / cruel mistress / bootlicker / jobsworth / test-tube baby yummy-mummy / yuppie scum / anti-vaxxer / trophy wife / here-for-a-good-time-not-a-long-time / do-you-have-a-light? / skintight / payload / homonym / i-have-work-tomorrow / cheat code / phone-it-in / neo-liberal / ex-catholic / leaking pipe / frankie-says-relax / lie-back-and-think-of-england / bonus track / urban myth / past-due / prosecco-flavoured / panic attack / panopticon / curbstomp / deck chair / semaphore / high-vis / give-'em-an-inch / kettling / do-you-hear-the-people-sing? / if-the-glove-fits / if-then / system flag / may-have-had-sex-with-a-man-who-may-have-had-sex-with-a-man / hypodermic / intravenous / transubstantiation / scientific method / wisdom teeth / bathroom stall / eurovision / cosmic latte / can-i-take-your-order-please? / alcoholic / vip / wall-to-wall / on the boil / hands up / i-don't-wanna-fight-tonight / baby-it's-cold-outside / two kids in a trenchcoat / pyromaniac / piggyback / you-spin-me-right-round / i-do-believe-in-fairies / don't-call-me-brave / feeling lucky / fire drill / union rep / back-in-my-day / what-can-i-say? / lick-it-up / i'm-not-bad-i'm-just-drawn-this-way / ekphrastic / biblically accurate / perfume advert / programming error / corporate espionage / do not resuscitate / education-education-education / section 28 / cursive / 5 GCSEs A*-C / your-name-here / day release / thought police / did-you-take-your-medication? / temporal paradox / meatsuit / messiah / mop and bucket / salt on the rim / strangler fig / depth charges / my-profit-on-it / supermarket own-brand / sugar-coated / swingers party / suburban monstrosity / fixer-upper / it-gets-better / point-on-the-diagram / scatter graph / outlier-who-should-not-have-been-counted / unexplained phenomena / gaping maw / astronaut / brilliant / brief / being

august in edinburgh
for bob

it's been dry for days now
but summer in scotland is the smell of wet leaves
and i have left you in the banshee
to pluck my tipsy way through midnight streets.

love isn't here yet
but every barefoot juggler catches in your cadence
and the glow of the circus tent
maps my path across this city drenched in song.

the breeze says return,
even as i spool the train tracks southward
and wind the year for winter.
i am listening to the wailing in my chest,

every station busker and magician
that points me the way i came, to this place,
and i am keeping august in my suitcase
like a promise, like a prayer.

compositional

at first the only place i wear it is to bed,
wade out into it like a roman bath, the spring of it
rumbling up from my bones, crystalline and fresh.
the cathedral of the human mouth has the best acoustics,
lingers on those wide open vowels, that *o*
you suck into those rounded depths the first note
in the chord of my name. i offer you this
so you can return it, call and response.
jonathan, a coin fed to the coffer during hymn,
sweet charity, blessed gift bestowed by the lord himself.
your tongue licks at the thorn in my middle, soothes
this unfathomable wound. i have not discarded love,
just cheap romance, these girlish trappings. i never
spoke the language, prefer a harsh germanic *n*
clipped and certain of its ends and its beginnings.

don't leave me this way

there's a place at the bottom of my mother's lungs
                        for the communards' cover,
      a belt, a shriek,
      a hallelujah over
                  those high notes, the steering wheel
                        her dance partner as she sings,
            her mouth so wide open
            i think her soul might fall out.

when i tell her
      her taste in music is pretty gay, she thinks a moment
      then says *i guess you're right* –

                        in my dad's car the cd player's
                        jammed full of stooges, bunnymen,
                              sex pistols,
            but i remember timing the ride to church
            in tracks of welcome to the pleasuredome,
            at six years old,
                  holly johnson's cackle rocking
                  my babyqueer bones,
                  an earthquake caught on record.

at that age,
      when i pictured dancers, i left out the thinness,
                        how their clothes ate them up:

      everyone looks pallid
                  under neon lights;
            everyone shakes like the spirit's entered them
                  in those disco cathedrals,
                        eats of the body,

(loves, loves, loves)
screams out their hymn:

don't leave me this way
don't leave me this way
don't leave me this way

boy

articulated as the vicar
plays captain hook, the pantomime,
                the wink and the nod of it —
how i know and he knows, we all know —
                he tastes,
                    swills his mouth with it.

boy,
            as in headmaster,
                as in officer,
                    as in no sir, wasn't i, sir,
                    belly down and holding my breath,

the sudden drag of his tongue
                        across the clitoris,
                    boy,
said with guilty-gleeful shudder,
                burning backside,

and the costume is coming off now,
        my cap in hand between my legs,
        my shorts around my ankles.
                            boy,

            like love,
                like being seen.

acknowledgements

many thanks to those without whom this body of work would not have come to fruition, i am forever in your debt. beyond the usual friends, family, lovers and tutors, I would specifically like to thank:

my sister, beatrix kinsman, for being the president of my fan club, sometimes making cool art of my poems, and knowing exactly when i need a cat depositing on my lap.

sam grudgings, for being my biggest influence, and putting up with me messaging him at midnight to ask if my poem sucks. he also invented the poetic form the corinthian and kindly allowed me to use it in a prayer of st. gertrude.

ian badcoe, casey bailey, lewis buxton, chris cambell, emilija ducks, pete green, maz hedgehog, jem henderson, kit ingram, aaron kent, john mccullough and jp seabright, for their editing help, mentoring, discussion of poetry and friendship. (and rose hoult, for knowing nothing about poetry but telling me that she liked it anyway).

kate garrett and matt mcateer, for being the very first to take a chance and offer me space in the world of poetry, on the page and stage respectively. i will see to it that i pay that kindness and faith forward at every opportunity.

dan holbrook, bob horton, kathy macy, gareth pedrick and snell, for everything. you know, just everything. i love you all very much.

and finally toby, my handsome, fluffy boy who never did anyone any harm, who saved my life, and who left me far too soon. i hope they have cheese wherever you have gone.

'a search party gathers after dark', 'three dreamscapes', and 'ghost sonnet for my vanishing twin' first appeared in *co-incidental 04: amy kinsman, megan pattie, rhys trimble, tom mccoll* (the black light engine room, 2019)

'birthday candles', 'otesanek (greedy guts)', 'some possible genders' and 'compositional' first appeared in *genederfux* (nine pens 2022), a pamphlet co-authored with jem henderson and jp seabright. 'some possible genders' was republished in *anthropocene* (2022)

'death of a boyband' first appeared in *the anatomy of desire: an anthology of distance* (the poetry annals, 2018)

'anton yelchin' first appeared in *prole #23* (2017) and was republished in the pamphlet *&* (indigo dreams 2018)

'bloodhound' first appeared online in *honey & lime* (2019)

'it's like this' and 'iterations of self' first appeared in the pamphlet *&* (indigo dreams 2018)

'how to walk on water' and 'on the electrodynamics of moving bodies' first appeared online in *bad lilies* (2023)

'levothyroxine' first appeared online in *the cardiff review's* queerly lit (2023)

'gravedigger' first appeared in the elements issue of *under the radar* (nine arches press, 2022)
'overture con sordina' first appeared in the anthology *tell me who we were before life made us* (3 of cups press, 2021)

'immolations' first appeared online in *kissing dynamite* (2019) and was nominated for the *best of the net* anthology 'werewulf' first appeared in *butcher's dog #13* (2020)

'elegy for a broken condom' first appeared in *fourteen poems #5* (2021)

the first section of 'transitional art forms' first appeared in *poetry wales* (2021)

'don't leave me this way' first appeared online in *glass poetry* (2019)

'boy' was shortlisted for the bridport prize for poetry (2022)

LAY OUT YOUR UNREST

www.ingramcontent.com/pod-product-compliance
Lightning Source LLC
LaVergne TN
LVHW041233080426
835508LV00011B/1192